Contents

Display and Presentation in Schools

CHRISTOPHER JARMAN

A & C BLACK LTD · LONDON

Acknowledgements

Grateful thanks are due to all those head-teachers and class teachers who so generously allowed their displays to be photographed. Especially to:

Francis Backhouse, Avery Baines, George Baines, Basil Benson, Philip Best, David Evans, Jim Griffiths, Sid Ing, Cliff Lassam, John Parker, Howard Probert, Joan Shields, Sue Simpkins and Nora Thomas.

The author and publishers also wish to thank the following Education Authorities for permission to use material from their schools:
Hampshire County Education Authority
Oxfordshire County Education Authority
Northampton County Borough Education
 Authority

The photograph on the cover shows children working at Ducklington County Primary School, Oxfordshire.

Published by A & C Black Ltd, 4 Soho Square, London W1V 6AD

© 1972 A & C Black Ltd

First published 1972

ISBN 0 7136 1295 9

Filmset by Photoset Ltd and printed in Great Britain by

Introduction

During the course of a busy day in school many teachers may feel that spending time on a careful display of interesting or stimulating materials is not worth the effort. One of the aims of this book is to convince both teachers and pupils that it is worthwhile.

The conditions in which we all spend our day have an important effect on our mood and efficiency, and on our attitudes. We need never be the victims of our surroundings. What we see around us each day in a classroom ought to be there by personal choice, like the decorations and objects in our own homes. We may not be able to control the seasons or the weather, or even to do much about the structure of the building, but we can still do a great deal to make our working environment artistically useful.

Every single photograph in this book has been taken in a genuine everyday situation in school. None of the displays was put up especially to be photographed. They are typical examples of what these teachers do, rather than perfected examples of display.

Since it is not always possible to get out of school to visit such places, it is hoped that the pictures in this book will serve as a kind of brief tour, and as a stimulus to anyone in school who feels like improving his own surroundings. Nothing expensive has been used, and all the materials are easily obtained.

Apart from making our working space more attractive, good display is a part of teaching. The aim is to show something so that it can be seen at its best. More and more teachers are concerned to give children first-hand experiences as an important part of exciting their interests.

The quality of children's own responses to museum exhibits, historical costume or even their own craft work, often depends on the care taken in displaying them. It is care and quality which are important here, for in the modern school where informality, flexibility and self-direction are such important values presentation becomes even more vital.

The formality and discipline of good displays present models for pupils to imitate. In this way high standards of layout, neat work and craftsmanship can be learnt in even the most flexible teaching situations. The teacher directs the children's attention to the displays around them, and ensures that they are *involved* in both understanding and creating them.

Obviously it would be impertinent for any person to try to teach good taste to another. Tastes change according to both fashion and the individual. This book shows a particular style of presentation, but it is by no means the only one.

Display can be crude, brazen and alarming. There are times when this should be so. Some subjects demand such treatment. In this book, however, we have tried to show how the everyday work of an ordinary school can be enriched. The objects we can bring into school are used as well as the work of the boys and girls themselves. We aim to make the walls, alcoves and spare spaces around us stimuli for learning.

Finally it must be affirmed most strongly that looking at a display is no substitute for action. 'Visual aid' alone is never enough to foster conceptual growth. The danger in only *showing* relationships in maths, or presenting models or historical weapons, is that mere percepts or images are formed. A good display is one that is used or touched, which starts a train of activities or which has resulted from the pupils' own practical activities. Only in this way will true concepts develop.

Colour

People planning a display often forget how important a part combinations of colour play in drawing attention. Colour can unify a set of objects which are quite different from one another but which you wish to group for a particular purpose. For example, if all hand-made pots were placed on a grey surface while all mass produced pots were put on a green surface, this in itself would help to unite the pieces in each set, while showing the difference between groups.

Brightly coloured displays of, say, Chinese models can be made to belong together if they share a plain background in a strong colour.

To focus attention on a particular item or part of any display, it is quite enough to cut a circle or any other shape out of a contrasting piece of coloured card or paper, and put the item on it. Small cylinders or boxes about 6 to 9 inches high and painted either in white or a quiet grey tone are also useful for lifting small objects from the flat surface and presenting them. Cylinders can be made from cardboard postal tubes or from card glued around coffee tins.

Halls, foyers and corridors

The effect of a dramatic and carefully arranged show of unusual and interesting materials can be breathtaking to a visitor coming into the school for the first time. The entrance lobby or foyer of any school may provide the chance to suggest the particular atmosphere that you want to create in the rest of the building.

It is an opportunity for the head in particular to exhibit his or her own interests and to set a standard and style of display for other teachers to follow. Many junior members of staff have been encouraged to make their own teaching areas more interesting through seeing the more public displays in entrance halls and corridors. The head, who often has no particular teaching area or classroom of his own, can make these parts of the school a vehicle for his skill as a presenter. In time other members of staff, and pupils, will feel able to use the hall and other open spaces for exhibitions as they become more confident.

This exhibition was photographed in a small corridor outside the headteacher's room in Ducklington County Primary School, Oxfordshire. The alcove was planned by the architect in consultation with the headmaster to be used for displays, and is faced in Cotswold stone with a plain wooden pelmet containing a concealed neon lighting unit.

Children's crafts from the school are shown mixed with adult craftwork. This indicates the value which the teaching staff put upon the work of the children, and indeed it is difficult to tell which is which. In fact the pots and the shepherd's crook are adult work; the batik pictures and the corn dollies were made by the children.

Exhibits remain on display here for three or four weeks at a time, and are borrowed by children to draw and measure and to use as a stimulus for writing.

Not all schools are fortunate enough to have a large hall. Where there is one, however, it provides a wonderful opportunity for display on a grand scale. In this school at Witney, the staff have used a corner of the hall to show work of all kinds done by children throughout the term. Good use has been made of height to drape tie-and-dye fabrics; and even the floor is used for displaying hand-made books, bound and covered.

Although there is a wide range of work, including textile crafts, hand-writing, bookcraft, mathematics, prose and poetry, drawings and paintings, a unity of display has been achieved through careful framing and positioning of the exhibits. Within this unity, variety has been used to keep the viewer's interest. The flat surfaces vary in height. A floor-level bay and the vertical column of card on the right arrest the eye. The choice of an L-shaped corner also helps, by ensuring a different light on each wall.

For the small school or the very old building, equally dramatic displays can be made on a small scale. The beautiful quality of these three stoneware pots, made by junior school children, is shown off by the plain wood against which they are placed.

Children are exposed to a great deal of crude and garish stimulus in town, on television, and often in the over-coloured and over-illustrated books and comics which they see. Their own classroom could be one of the few places where subtle, quiet tones are presented to them. This can be as restful to the eye as a country walk is to the ear.

There is no need for your display to stand on the usual sugar paper or formica top. It is well worth buying some lengths of material to keep and use as textured backings. A fine maize mat about six feet by three feet is an invaluable natural texture backing. Here it is used to display wood blocks for fabric printing, made by eleven year old girls.

Undyed lengths of woollen cloth, hessian, unbleached calico or linen are also very good as groundcloths or backcloths. A large roll of clean hessian can be stretched over a row of desks to transform them into a crisp and professional looking display table.

Classification displays

In many schools, and especially in the 5–9 age range, collections are often put out showing objects or materials which share something in common. If carefully thought out, these can be very important teaching aids. Apart from the pleasure which collections of any kind always seem to give people of all ages, such families of objects help young children to understand the materials of the world around them. Some six and seven year olds are not sure what is metal, and what is, say, porcelain. Collections of each can help them to establish from first-hand experience which is which.

This collection of glassware was displayed by the staff of a primary school in Bicester. The children can see and touch articles of all kinds made of glass. They have also been encouraged to take pieces away and draw them, measure them, discover their capacities, and so on. As the days pass, the empty spaces on the corrugated card backing will fill up with the children's work inspired by the exhibits.

The teachers will have taken small groups to the display and pointed out certain qualities as discussion points. Questions will stimulate further thought. How much water do you think the big carboy will hold? What would the container with bumps on be used for? Why do the wine bottles have straw round them? Which piece is designed to float in water? Can you see two glasses of different sizes but similar shape? How many glassfuls would fill that large one?

On the opposite page you can see part of a classifying display in the entrance hall of Hamble Primary School in Hampshire.

Young children today need to be reminded of the basic materials which have served man's technology through history and which continue to do so—glass, metal, wood and clay. Here the pottery, bricks, sewer pipe and flower pot are all made from the earth itself.

Other examples of classifying displays often seen are: different objects and materials in shades of one colour; sea shells and shellfish; building materials—bricks, slates and tiles; tools; paperwork and paper varieties; various metals, cast iron, steel and so on; weaving of all types; dyed textiles; hand-made wooden articles; weapons and armour; domestic objects from a particular period in history, for example Tudor or Victorian.

Nowadays museums and museum school loan services are offering more and more collections to schools and you can take advantage of these. In certain areas parents and local families can be a valuable source of collection material for loan. Old toys, games and wartime souvenirs have been borrowed and used to start some good work. Old farm implements or the tools of a rural craftsman are fascinating to children.

The reason behind all such classifying displays is, of course, to help children to see the relatedness of various families, groups and sets of things. In this way abstraction and

generalisation of the whole concept of 'tool', 'clay', 'weaving', and so on, becomes possible. And there is always the possibility that a good collection may start a new interest.

Use has been made of the floor space for this display. Cream sugar paper has been simply laid around the base of a plywood stage block, up-ended and draped with unbleached calico.

Woodcarving in an Oxfordshire school

Labelling

Most labelling on displays tends to spoil their effectiveness. If a show is well planned, particularly if it contains some of the children's own written work, labels can be avoided altogether. A good display communicates by itself.

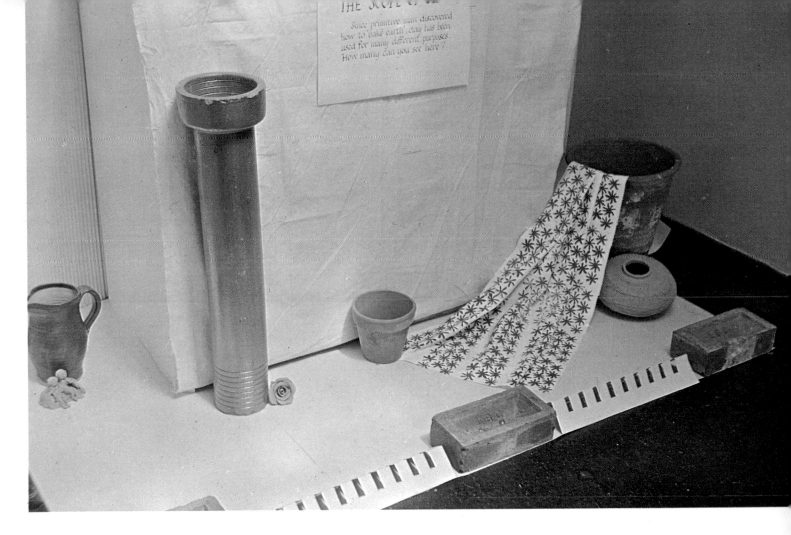

When some sort of writing has to be added, the card should be white, or light in colour, and the ink black or perhaps a dark shade matching the main display colours. If all the labels are the same size and shape, and placed in line with one another, a better and more unified effect can be achieved.

Either plain Roman capitals or a good foundation hand is best. Unless done by a trained calligrapher, flourished lettering looks amateurish and unsightly. Poorly lettered labels are becoming rare these days, with letraset, typewriters and stencils available.

Do bear in mind that labels have to be read easily, possibly by small children if your display is in a primary school. Keep them low down, at a child's eye level.

The following labels appear on the cards in the display:

skull   bone
jaw   leg
teeth   head
eye socket
shoulder blade
vertebrae   back
rib   tail
chest

joint
ball and socket
hinge
knee
foot
spinal cord
muscle

Starting an interest

It would be hard to avoid starting an interest in an infants' school with a display like this of a real human skull and various bones!

This dramatic corner is in a hutted classroom in Oxfordshire. The teacher has chosen a stark black background of card, and covered two levels with black pastel paper to emphasize the outlines of the bones. This particular display was especially striking, because the alcove had been made to face anyone entering the classroom door.

What many adults may consider old junk can be drawn upon by the sensitive and knowledgeable teacher. An imaginative leap into the past can be encouraged by handling an old key, and talking about it. How many poor serving girls used and polished those old fire-tongs? What was it like to read in bed with this little oil lamp? How did they make corn dollies and why?

With the real objects piled there beside them in their own classroom, children have a genuine desire to know the answers to such questions. This is a disorderly display, but deliberately so, because the exhibits are there to be picked up, to stimulate, to excite and arouse the imagination. By handling and discussing these real things from the past, children who are still at the stage of concrete thinking may get a little nearer to putting themselves in the place of those who used to handle them. One child who found the fingerprint of a Roman potter on a bowl suddenly realised that the ancient Romans were ordinary people like us.

Handling history itself

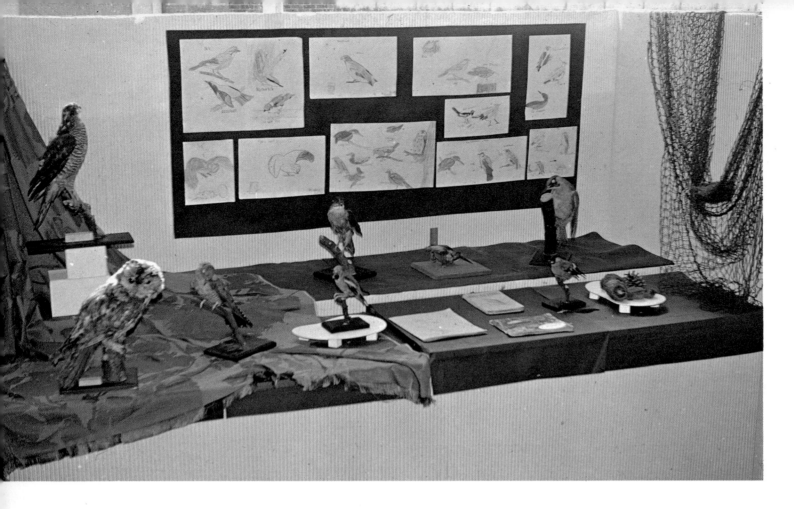

Display space within the classroom is often very limited indeed. In some modern buildings there is so much window area that one is forced to cover up some of the glass. Here a young teacher in a junior school near Southampton has used a spare dining table and white corrugated card placed against the window to start an interest in bird life.

The stuffed birds were borrowed from a museum which was understanding enough not to enclose them in transparent cases.

Small plywood boxes, painted white, are useful props, and two have been used to create more height for the bird of prey on the left. A nest is shown hanging in the netting, and the beginnings of the children's work are pinned at the back.

Notice how the table is given a more solid appearance by a skirting of corrugated card. No distracting tacks are showing because black paper has been turned down over the front edge and secured by dressmaker's pins

This is the corner of a modern classroom at Spring Lane Primary School, Northampton. The display was set up by a student on her first teaching practice. Although as an aesthetic display it lacks finish and precision, it was an excellent stimulus for children's work and led to a very fruitful study of the Grand Union Canal nearby. The student teacher went to a great deal of trouble to find authentic canal furniture, paintings and pots, and to make work cards directing the children's activities. A film and a visit to the canal was part of the scheme. This kind of stimulus can do so much to make both the teacher's and the children's day more enjoyable and interesting; yet often it is done on teaching practices only!

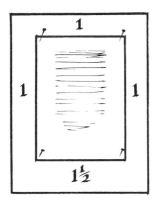
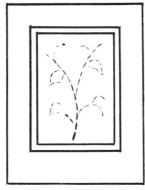

Left: *single mounting. The picture or writing may be glued or pinned with four small dressmaker's pins through mounting card or backing. Suitable margin proportions are shown*

Right: *double mounting. First glue or pin the exhibit to a black or contrasting colour paper, about 1 cm larger all round. The two sheets are then treated as a single mount*

Presentation and mounting

The first requirement in the presentation of children's work is that the children themselves value their own product and present it well. This will not happen unless:

a. the work is completely the child's own— his own choice of subject and his own untouched effort;

b. the skills of presenting work well have been *taught*, including good handwriting, good bookmaking, sensitive use of drawing materials, an understanding of framing, and margin proportions.

The desire to match up to a teacher's expectations is a strong motive for producing neat work.

It has been observed in many schools where high standards of presentation are expected, that the children have marked self-discipline and deep involvement in their work. In an open-plan situation in particular, such expectations seem to provide a unifying factor in even the most flexible of organisations.

Various ways of folding and standing corrugated card

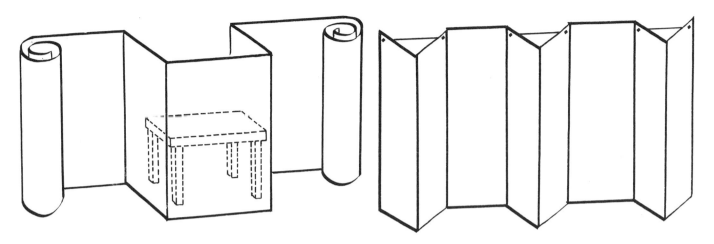

Fold round a table, chair or stage to make a buttress

V-pillars give more area for display in a small space

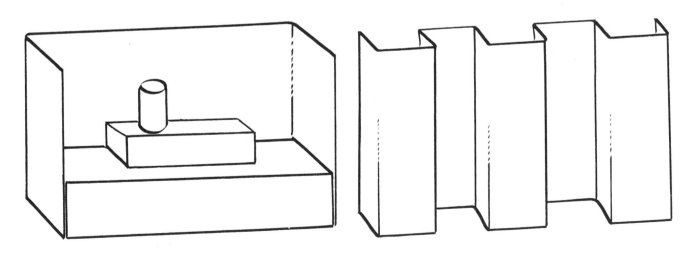

Alcove around stage blocks or a table

Square pillars help to break up a large flat wall area

Work done by children

One common difficulty in showing the work of a class is finding enough space to put up every child's effort. The penalty of overcrowding is a fussy display, with one piece overlapping another and some left unmounted.

The photograph on the opposite page shows how a young teacher tackled this problem with a class of eight year olds. At the back of the classroom, above the radiator, a roll of six foot corrugated card has been pinned and unrolled around the corner right across the large window which runs the whole length of the room. The other two sides of this room are almost all glass, so very little light was lost. Nearly a hundred examples of work are displayed on these two walls alone. Each piece is mounted on black sugar paper. The work is pinned to the mounts so that they can be used over and over again.

Several of the children's handbound books are lying on the workbench and a touch display of objects found in the sea is in the corner. Tie-and-dye work is laid out on the table.

The artwork on display is carefully arranged in vertical rectangles, each section showing the different technique used.

1. Finger painting
2. Examples of symmetry by painting or folding
3. String prints
4. Pattern painting
5. Chalk drawings of botanical specimens, using lenses for close observation
6. Paste combing
7. Pastel designs
8. Patterns made by blowing wet paint with milk straws

This was a simple way of exhibiting the work of a class after they had been cutting paper patterns. The display is pinned to a scroll of card standing in a corridor.

This is a starkly effective way of decorating a dull piece of wall. Particularly where the light is poor, a black and white design such as this can be seen more clearly than one dependent on subtle shades. In this case a group of juniors had been glueing white wool on to black paper, making pictures quite independently of one another. Then the pictures were brought together to make a rather charming mural.

The teacher's insistence on retaining a rectangle gave the design an overall cohesion.

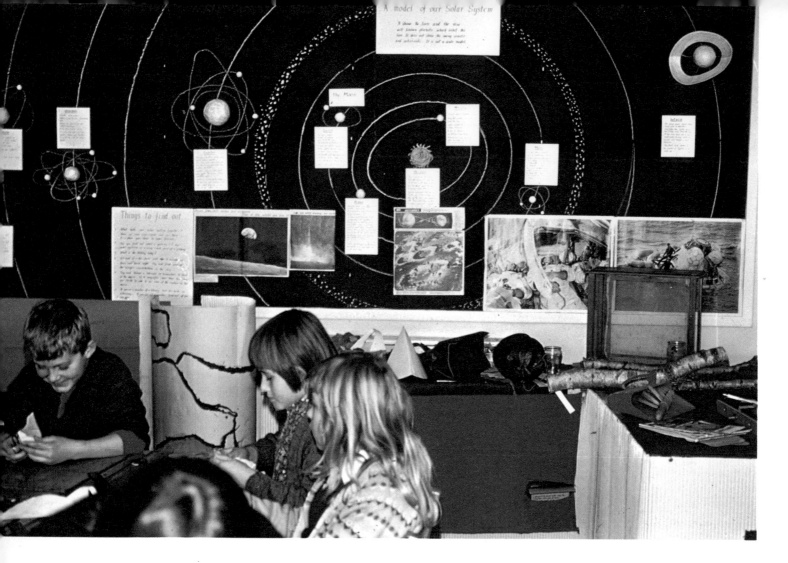

The type of display which is built up slowly as the work develops has already been mentioned. Here is another interesting example. The class had been working on a space project connected with one of the moon landings. As a child found some information about the components of the solar system, so the board was built up and the planets placed in their positions. White chalk on black sugar paper shows their orbits. The whole is a kind of bulletin board reference display.

Nooks and crannies

What is it that distinguishes the professionally outstanding classroom from the merely good one? It is certainly not a question merely of tidiness or interesting walls. Nor is peace and quiet a necessary ingredient; a hum of purposeful activity may signify more.

One feature is the economic use of space; another is the rich provision of well-used books and materials. I would also suggest that the imaginative use of odd corners and small spaces is another indication of the highly competent practitioner, and so is the care with which even the most mundane of tasks is done. When a group of children finish their work and put it on one side before going home, it is rewarding to find a corner of their classroom looking like the one in the photograph.

> Everything beckons us to perceive it,
> Murmurs at every turn, 'Remember me!'
> A day we passed, too busy to receive it,
> Will yet unlock to us all its treasury.
>
> RAINER MARIA RILKE

Small displays in the corners of the school should beckon us to touch them. It is a sad fact, however, that many children have already been allowed to take or break anything that is touchable before reaching school age. How far a teacher can encourage touch displays depends on the atmosphere created in the school. Recent experience suggests that even in an area well known for a

Mosaics of natural grains

generally high level of juvenile delinquency, certain schools are able to establish excellent trusting relationships within their own communities. In any truly educational situation some risks must be taken—but preferably without jeopardising anything irreplaceable!

Touch displays

A touch display is usually a collection of natural objects which will repay close study. The educational value of such collections for young children is that they foster discrimination by encouraging the use of the sense of touch as well as the senses of sight and smell. Many little children need to be taught such words as

spiny	hard	brittle
prickly	shiny	pointed
spongey	soft	convex
tacky	velvet	concave
serrated	sharp	rough
hollow	smooth	pitted

and with touch displays this aspect of language can be taught in context while the relevant surfaces are being fingered.

With older children, who are entering the stage of more concrete thinking, close observation of natural things such as stones, rocks, fossils, coral, shells, bones, seed pods, plants, skeletons and so on, provides some of the essential perceptual experiences which form part of the bricks and mortar of intellectual development.

Detailed drawing and painting, stemming from sustained close observation is, in the view of many teachers, helping to make children more accurate and articulate in expression. Marion Richardson rightly released children from the drudgery of mere copywork, and lifeless plant drawing from the

blackboard. Large murals, and dramatic emotive painting are a rich part of our schoolwork today. Lately, however, the orderly discipline of studying the infinite patterns of nature has been recognised as an activity complementary to other forms of artwork. The whole subject of orderly display is bound up with the same values—craftsmanship, simplicity and respect for materials.

Craftsmanship and simplicity are seen in many old hand-made implements and devices. This waggon wheel from the Woodstock Museum in Oxfordshire is not part of a display. It *is* the display in itself. The dramatic intrusion of such a large, heavy thing into the classroom is provoking and exciting to the children. The wheel was placed in a maths workbay because it was the largest example of a circle in the room, and a good deal of work on circles developed from this particular wheel. Nevertheless, its value as an object of good, functional craftsmanship was also being pointed out by the teacher.

Bernard Leach has quoted the words of a Japanese craftsman: 'Simplicity may be thought of as a characteristic of cheap things, but it must be realised that it is a quality that harmonises well with beauty.'

One should beware of becoming too precious and stylised in the approach to displays. A large dirty lump of coal and a sweaty miner's helmet, which I once saw in a West Riding primary school, has stayed in my mind ever since.

As something to touch and to wonder at, even to play with, as well as to provide starting points for maths, history, art and environmental study topics, this wheel can hardly be bettered.

Boldness is the essence of good display

Tucked away in the same classroom as the wheel, this teacher had put out a selection of shells, books of reference, and even some English slipware pottery which depended on designs from the sea. Once more, children were being invited to touch and take away both shells and books to study, and to match the shell with its picture. Lenses were provided nearby for more detailed observation.

The patterns in artwork need not be the repetitive and often thoughtless doodles so often seen on classroom walls, but strong natural designs based upon the children's experience of reality, and heightened by their imaginations and that of their teacher.

The ability to create abstract patterns in adolescence or adulthood depends upon the food provided by the endless patterns of natural materials in the child's early experiences. True imagination and creativity stem from being able to select and rekindle the apparently new from a rich storehouse of past actions. Without the input of looking, and even sometimes copying, in order to remember, no future artistic or intellectual output is possible. It may sound unfashionable to recommend careful copying today, but it is sound sense. All artists know it!

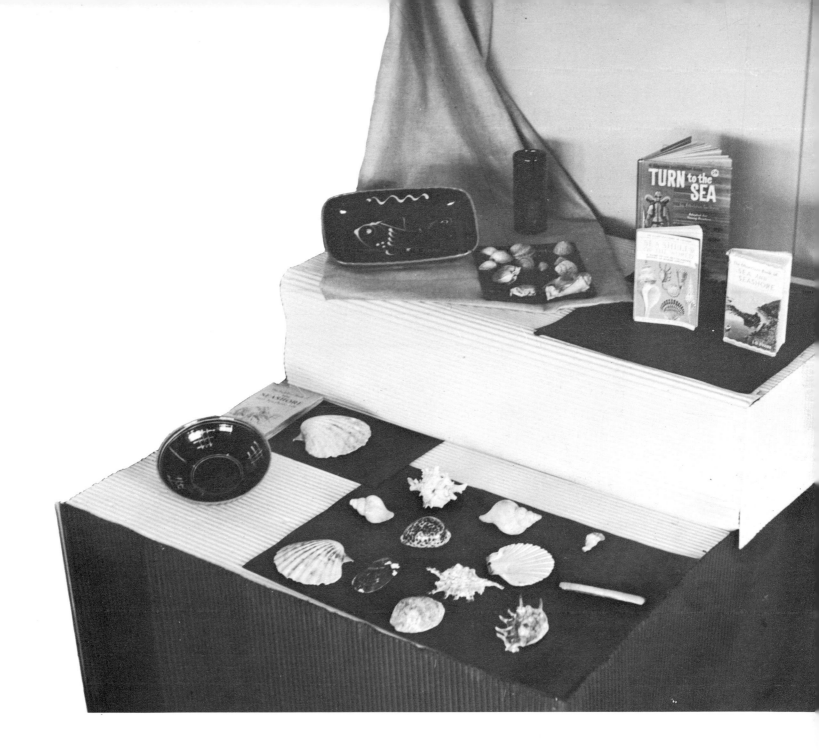

Shelves

As soon as one sees shelves in the classroom it is tempting to fill them with rows of books or to use them as mere storage spaces. Nevertheless, even under the most cramped conditions, many teachers manage to set aside some shelves for the sole purpose of making the room more pleasant to live in. Here beautiful natural objects brought in by an infant teacher are both stored and presented in a pleasing way.

Children presenting their own work

This section of an 18th Century street scene is part of a mural being gradually assembled by a small group of ten year olds. It is shown because it is entirely the children's own work and was put up by them as their own developing display. It began through one of their teachers bringing into school some very old Chinese figures, made by glueing fabric onto flat cardboard shapes. Some of the girls copied them, and others said they would rather make figures of ladies in hooped skirts, and searched the illustrated history books for correct designs.

Another teacher then took a group of children out to look at some Georgian streets. Drawings were made, and on their return, cut-out silhouettes of the houses were done with sharp knives, rulers and various shades of sugar paper. The idea of a street in which to put the figures was a natural follow up.

This eight year old is putting a calligraphic border around a piece of her own writing which is to be displayed on the wall. By pattern-making she is learning to design, and she is practising her own handwriting skills

When good handwriting and presentation is continually shown to young children, they naturally begin to imitate what they see. In the modern, more flexible approach to learning, good layout provides an intrinsic self-discipline which has a calming orderly effect upon the atmosphere of an open plan or 'workshop' style of school.

After making aprons from their own lino printed fabrics, ten year olds in a Hampshire school decided to display them as if on a washing line for a parents' evening—a simple but unusual idea which the teacher admitted he would never have thought of himself!

In a corner of a junior school classroom, two children have made a small exhibition of their own work. They have been following interests common among the 9–11 age group, horses and birds. Here the teacher has encouraged them to set out the final outcome of their small studies as an encouragement and stimulus to others.

Where the age range is mixed, this sort of display is very useful in providing both interests and aims for the younger children. Where pupils see careful displays set up by the adults around them, they take their cue from the standards that are set.

All these activities give a style to the interior of a school and provide novelty and change, which ensures that neither the teachers nor the children become bored with their surroundings.

Bibliography

ASHBRIDGE, WA *The Display and Care of Books in Primary Schools*, School Library Association (Premier House, 150 Southampton Row, London WC1). This is a useful small pamphlet.

CORBIN, TJ *Display in Schools*, Pergamon.

EAST, M & DALE, E *Display for Learning*, Holt Rinehart & Winston.

LAMB, CM *The Calligrapher's Handbook*, Faber.

LEGGAT, R *Showing off, or Display Techniques for the Teacher*, National Committee for Audio-Visual Aids in Education (33 Queen Anne Street, London W1M 0AL).

The corner of a classroom in Stoke Park County Junior School,
Hampshire. This display was prepared by the children
themselves

Materials and Suppliers

Background materials

Rolls of corrugated card are obtained in 36 yard lengths, height 5ft 10in, in various colours including white, grey, black, yellow and red, from:

The English Corrugated Paper Co Ltd, Portland Square, Bristol.

Hessian, unbleached cotton and various fabrics used in embroidery and needlework make excellent drapes and backcloths, and are available from:

Dryad Ltd, Northgate, Leicester

or from:

Nottingham Handicraft Company, Melton Road, West Bridgford, Nottingham.

Interesting background fabrics, such as woven wheat straw, Japanese grass paper, silver grey hessian, are available from:
Primavera, 17 Walton Street, London SW3.

Handmade papers, pastel papers and various types of card in white or colours from:

T N Lawrence & Son Ltd, 2 Bleeding Heart Yard, Greville Street, London EC1

and from:

Hunt and Broadhurst, Botley Road, Oxford

as well as most good educational suppliers.

Display screens and structures

The Marler Haley multiscreen system is one of the best and most adaptable ready-made systems. It consists of hessian faced screens in various sizes which interlock to form backboards, shelves, racks and exhibition stands of all kinds. The system is tasteful, strong and durable. Fully illustrated catalogues and price list from:

Marler Haley (Barnet) Ltd, 76 High Street, Barnet, Hertfordshire.

Buckley Displays Ltd produce lightweight pinboards made from expanded polystyrene covered with coloured hessian. They also provide wall fittings, or stands, as well as chalkboards. Leaflets and colour swatch for 'Buckboard' (there is a wide range of attractive colours) are available from:

Buckley Displays Ltd, 5 Clevemede House, Reading, RG8 9BX.

Pegboards and accessories

Pegboards, being a regular and mechanical design, are not aesthetically pleasing as a background, but can be used for displaying tools and books and for storage racks. Pegboard is available from many sources, including:

E J Arnold & Son Ltd, Butterley Street, Leeds 10.

Other pegboard fittings can be obtained from:
M Myers & Son Ltd, PO Box 16, Oldbury, Warley, Worcestershire.

Display racks for books

For wooden, metal, pegboard and wire display stands of all kinds, a firm which produces a full catalogue of library equipment is:
Librex Educational Company, Meadow Lane, London Road, Nottingham, NG23HS.

Paper for brass rubbings etc

The paper called in Dryad's catalogue 'Smooth Printing Paper' is excellent for rubbings of all sorts. W H Smith sell rolls of shelf lining paper which is also cheap and good. But for best quality rubbings, use detail paper, obtainable from artists' and architects' suppliers.

Glues and adhesives

Copydex is the most universally useful as it can be used to stick corrugated card to painted white walls and will come off without causing damage.

Cow gum is excellent for mounting delicate work on card. It is a rubber solution and can be removed by applying a little petrol (lighter fuel) with a fine brush and gradually peeling away the picture from the mount. Available from stationers, or from:

P B Cow (Li-Lo Ltd), Slough, Bucks

Plasti-tak is an unusual and useful addition. Used rather like chewing gum, it will stick anything on the wall, from a woodcarving to a photograph. Full instructions come with the pack. A thousand uses in display work. Its virtue is that it can be used over and over again. From:

Philip & Tacey Ltd, 69 Fulham High Street, London SW6.

Tools

A pin pusher is an essential piece of equipment; with it you can avoid using large-headed drawing pins. Available from:

Thomas & Easter, 23a George Street, Baker Street, London W1.

Lettering pens can be bought in fountain pen sets with several sizes of screw-in nib units, from:

E S Perry Ltd, Osmiroid Works, Fareham Road, Gosport, Hants

or from:

Platignum Ltd, Stevenage, Herts.

For display work which is to be very large, with lettering up to six or nine inches high,

a Boxall or automatic pen is most appropriate. These are obtainable from:

G M Dupont, 23 Westland Court, Fishergate, Portslade, Sussex,

or from any first class stationers.

A large guillotine and a small card cutter are needed to ensure that children's work can be trimmed before mounting. Also a good deal of time is saved in making mounts. From most educational suppliers.

Staple guns

These are useful in some circumstances but remember that someone has to extract the staples eventually! Staples show up less than drawing pins and are thus more discreet for display work. The 'Trigger Tacker', from E J Arnold, is a good alternative to a staple gun.

Italic handwriting

The Society for Italic Handwriting is international and publishes a useful quarterly journal of interest to teachers. The subscription is £1·20 pa (US $3) for adults, and 40p pa (US $1) for those under eighteen.

Enquiries or initial subscriptions should be sent to:

The Secretary, 41 Montpelier Rise, Wembley, Middlesex.

Inks

Brusho powdered inks from Duckett's can be mixed to any colour and safely used in a fountain pen. Beware of waterproof inks as they clog pens and nibs. From:

J B Duckett & Co, 74 Broadfield Road, Sheffield 8.

A good black ink for writing and lettering which may be used in a fountain pen and is available from most stationers is:

Pelican Fount-India.

Manufactured lettering

Plastic letters and boarding from:

PIP Publicity Ltd, Imperial House, Little Newton Street, Manchester 4.

Boards and soft adhesive PVC letters, numerals, etc, from:

Zell-em Ltd, 210 Watson Road, Blackpool, Lancashire.

Letraset, Letterpress, or other brands of instant lettering, are available from any office stationers, or from E J Arnold. Catalogues of typefaces for the different brands are available.